TALKS
TO
SEE

Compiled by
Albert L. Zobell, Jr.

Published by
Deseret Book Company
Salt Lake City, Utah
1971

Library of Congress No. 77-155236
SBN No. 87747-436-2

Lithographed by

DESERET NEWS PRESS

in the United States of America

DEDICATION
To you and to yours.
May *Talks to See* always light your way.

TABLE OF CONTENTS

Did You Ever Try?

Items Needed

A dry sponge, a pan of water.

Action During Presentation

Keep the sponge dry to begin with. Squeeze it and have it passed to members of the group for squeezing to show that a dry sponge gives out nothing. Later submerge the sponge in the water, letting it soak as much as possible. Squeeze the water out of the sponge back into the pan.

Suggested Wording for Presentation

Did you ever try to get water out of a sponge? (Pass it around.) We shall let all who desire to do so, try it. You cannot squeeze water out of the dry sponge; we all know it is impossible.

The only way to ever get water out of a sponge is to put the water into the sponge in the first place. (Soak sponge in water.) Now, who would like to try again? (Demonstrate)

This truth makes itself known in our preparation for almost anything in life—especially for teaching the gospel. We must first thoroughly soak up our preparation before, sponge-like, we can take the "living water" from ourselves to give to others.

Activity Is the Moving Force

Items Needed

Postage stamps, envelopes

Action During Presentation:

You will develop this thought around three actions: 1. Addressing the letter; 2. Placing one cent stamp on letter; 3. Adding additional postage stamps; 4. Showing additional air and special delivery stamps.

Suggested Wording for Presentation

Activity is the life's blood of any organization. Every member whose goal is eternal life needs activity to gain it. How can you attain it?

First: You must know where you want to go. If you were to send this letter to a friend in a distant town, you would need to write the name on the envelope, have the address, the town, state, and zip code. But even with all that, if you put your letter in the nearest mailbox, what would happen? Your precious letter would be returned to you or go to the dead letter office. Why? Because you forgot to put some authority, some activity upon it. It needs a postage stamp on it to even start it off in the direction of the goal that you intend to achieve.

Second: So it needs a stamp—some authority, some action to get it going. What kind of stamp or stamps do you intend to place on it? You can still buy a stamp for a penny, and they may still make half-cent stamps. You can be barely active—a penny's worth. One of your most precious gifts in mortality is your free agency. But what is going to happen if you put a one-cent stamp on your envelope and drop it into the nearest mailbox? How far is it going to go? How far are you going to go towards eternal life with one-cent activity?

Third: You will need full postage to get your letter to its destination; just as you need full activity to get yourself to the Kingdom. Even then, the post office handles letters in several ways. First class surface mail is most satisfactory to many. Add a five-cent stamp to the one-cent stamp and your letter will arrive where you want it to go. Add first class activity to your Church service and you too may arrive where you want to.

Fourth: For a little more you can use an air-mail stamp; or added activity in the form a special delivery stamp can insure that your letter reaches its intended goal in the fastest possible time.

What kind of stamps—what kind of activity—will you use? It is recorded by Luke:

". . . a certain lawyer stood up and tempted Jesus saying, Master, what shall I do to inherit eternal life?

He said unto him, What is written in the law? how readest thou?"

"And he answering said, Thou shalt love the Lord thy God with all thy heart, and with all thy soul, and with all thy strength, and with all thy mind: and thy neighbour as thyself."

"And he said unto him, Thou hast answered right: this do, and thou shalt live." (Luke 10:25-28.)

Adverse Winds

Item Needed

An icicle from a nearby roof. Bring it in a bottle.

Action During Presentation:

Call attention to the shape of the icicle; after the icicle has been examined, call attention to the discolored water in the bottle.

Suggested Wording for Presentation

The Apostle Paul touched upon our subject today in Ephesians 4:14:

"That we henceforth be no more children, tossed to and fro, and carried about with every wind of doctrine, by the sleight of men, and cunning craftiness, whereby they lie in wait to deceive."

You will note the shape of the icicle in this bottle. It could have been bent and twisted out of shape as the wind drove the forming water before it.

So is the human character, like this icicle, formed, bent, or shaped by the winds that blow upon it. Those winds might be in our modern age of going with the crowd that persistently chooses the wrong way to go; the winds might be habits that turn us from the right path; or other influences that keep us from growing straight and true.

You will notice also that the icicle is discolored, as is the water that has melted from it. The icicle was only made up of the discoloring elements that went into it. So with men and women—they are made up of the elements that go into forming their characters and lives.

Over the centuries we hear the scripture thunder:

"Be ye clean who bear the vessels of the Lord."
(Isa. 52:11.)

Are We Preparing?

Items Needed

A partially open door.

Action During Presentation

If the door used is a cardboard or plastic (etc.,) replica, it could be made as a swinging door. As you talk about doors swinging on hinges without purpose, demonstrate with the door in swinging action and when you talk about opening doors with purpose control the action of the door with possible handle.

Suggested Wording for Presentation

Did you ever try to sleep on a windy night? There was not much sleep if a swinging door was caught by the wind and was kept swinging. What a wild wind can and does do with a door such as this.

Did you ever liken the movement of something in all that wind to the haphazard direction that our lives sometimes take, as we apparently lose sight, just for a moment, of our final goal, and go pursuing "every wind of doctrine"? How we are likened to a swinging door.

Doors are useful. A door opens and closes for us. As we walk through an open door we find ourselves in a different environment. New opportunities open to us as we walk through an open door; sadness and disappointment are sometimes closed to us as we close a door.

But what good is a door that merely swings on its hinges? All that wasted energy.

Speaking to the Saints assembled in the Bowery on Temple Square for general conference, October 6, 1863, President Brigham Young counselled:

"Brethren and sisters, are we preparing for the highest seat of knowledge and literature known to men on earth, and then to go on in advance of them by the means of the Spirit bestowed upon us in the ordinances of our holy religion, which reveals all things, and thus become ourselves teachers and expounders of . . . the kingdom of God on earth and in heaven? Would not this be much better than to remain fixed with a very limited amount of knowledge, and, like a door upon its hinges, move to and fro from one year to another without any visible advancement or improvement, lusting after the grovelling things of this life which perish with the handling? Let each one of us bring these matters home to ourselves." (Journal of Discourses 10:266.)

As a Man Thinketh

Items Needed

A five cent piece.

Action During Presentation

Place the five cent piece over the eye, close the other eye, so that the vision is entirely blocked by the money.

Suggested Wording for Presentation

It is recorded: "For as [a man] thinketh in his heart, so is he." (Prov. 23:7.)

We do not know what kind of man the writer of the Proverbs had in mind. How is your sense of values? Are you one to permit one nickel, or one line of thought, to block your view of everything else that is good to see in the world?

What would you surrender for the sake of money? This five cent piece, for instance? Perhaps you would not surrender very many values for just this nickel. But it is possible to bring this small nickel closer and closer to the eye until you can see absolutely nothing else. Unfortunately many have done just that, although a few have set out deliberately to accomplish just that.

While the five cent piece may not be or seem to be very much, the idea of what it does to a person is what really counts. If it fills your vision, if it fills your thoughts, if it becomes of paramount importance to you, it may warp your vision or your thinking or your sense of values for anything higher in life.

There is a challenge in the Sermon on the Mount: "For where your treasure is, there will your heart be also." (Matt. 6:21.)

How is your sense of values?

As We Comply

Items Needed

You will need one or two electric cords, with lamp extensions. You will need a low-powered light globe and a greater strength light globe.

Action During Presentation

As you proceed with the discussion you will want to turn on the low powered electric light and then the greater strength of light. They may be turned off and on according to the discussed points.

Suggested Wording for Presentation

The words "light" and "truth" are often used interchangeably in the scriptures. They are used together in the Doctrine and Covenants, section 93, verses 36 and 37:

"The glory of God is intelligence, or, in other words, light and truth.

"Light and truth forsake that evil one." (D. & C. 93: 36-37.)

The intelligence of God, or the light and truth of the gospel, is available to all of us. How do we get more of that light into our lives? It depends entirely on us. As receivers and dispensers of the light and truth, our capacity is conditioned by our ability to live closely to the principles of the gospel. As we understand and obey the teachings, we become able to contain and radiate more of the truth and light of the gospel.

This little demonstration may help explain this truth. These electrical cords carry the electrical current so common in our lives. Electricity taken from such wires as these can and does provide refrigeration, cooking, entertainment through television, stereo, radio, light to read by, and many other important tasks.

As the need demands we may turn on a low powered light, for less current, or a stronger powered light for more current.

The power of the light of God is there also at our bidding, as we comply with the laws that make it available to us. We need only to turn the switch—or to obey—to receive what current we want. Are we going to be content with the low powered light, or do we prefer to bring the greater powered light into play in our lives?

We are the ones to prepare ourselves for whatever spiritual light we desire. Are we satisfied with none at all, or a very small light, or would we prefer a great deal of light? The power is there, depending on our own preparation and bidding.

At First Glance It Is A Glamorous Life

Items Needed

A string puppet or marionette.

Action During Presentation

Puppet should be performing smoothly and easily; then jerked or upset as the strings are pulled; then collapsed as the strings become entangled.

Suggested Wording for Presentation

How would you like to be a puppet? At first glance it looks like a glamorous life. You would always be the center of attention, performing in the spotlight, receiving the applause from the crowd.

But what are these strings? Oh, if you were a puppet, someone else would control your every action, merely by pulling the strings. Would you really like that?

This was Lucifer's plan presented to us in the pre-existence. His plan would not permit free agency during earth's sojourn. He and his demands would pull the strings on our every action.

And see how easy these strings get entangled. If we had a high-speed camera we could see how one string gets out of line and in a twinkling all the strings are entangled. That is a lot like getting entangled in sin. Once we are entangled in sin we must stop such activity, sit quietly down, and through repentance, disentangle ourselves.

But each of us here chose a way different from Lucifer's puppets. In the pre-existence we voted for the plan of the Christ and free agency. It is written by John that Jesus said:

"If ye continue in my word, then are ye my disciples indeed;

"And ye shall know the truth, and the truth shall make you free." (John 8:31-32.)

To be disciples of Jesus Christ is to be eternally free.

At Least Two Ways of Sharing

Items Needed

Two frosted and decorated cakes. Perhaps only one should be in view at the beginning. Plate, napkin, fork.

Action During Presentation

When the discussion calls for the action, plunge hand into cake and offer a handful of cake to the class. Secondly, cut piece neatly, place on plate, serve with fork and napkin.

Suggested Wording for Presentation

There are often two ways of doing everything—two ways of serving cake, two ways of teaching the gospel, two ways of giving a gift to a friend, two ways of sharing a truth.

"Would you like some cake? Why, of course, you would."

Plunge your hand into the cake, scoop a large handful, and offer it to the class. Oh, oh.

Would you like to try that again?

This time cut a small piece of the cake, place it on the plate, and with napkin and fork, offer the cake to the class.

Two ways of serving cake—which one is to be preferred? There are also two ways of teaching the gospel, and two ways of sharing truth. How do you go about the divine injunction of missionary work—that most rewarding activity of sharing the gospel, and by so doing seeing your own understanding and appreciation of it grow?

The gospel must be presented and shared in such a way that it is desirable (and it certainly is) to our non-member friends. The truths that Jesus gave to us must be understood and taught and given to our friends in "appetizing" form, in courteous yet appealing ways.

There are two ways to do most everything. Which way do you choose?

Don't Clog the Mechanism

Items Needed

An alarm clock, some dirty thick oil.

Action During Presentation

The action will not be actual; but showing the alarm clock and the oil, act as though you would pour the dirty oil into the mechanism of the alarm clock.

Suggested Wording for Presentation

This is a faithful alarm clock. Many times it has sounded off at its appointed time in the morning. Many times it has started its owner off in the direction he should be going and at the time he should be going as well.

The alarm clock has served faithfully and well; it may not look too good, but it is still ticking loud and clear. What would happen if we should dump some of this dirty oil into its works? How long would it then continue to tick loud and clear and faithfully?

It may need oil, but it needs the right kind of oil. Would anyone deliberately clog the mechanism of such an alarm clock? Not if he wanted to keep it in good condition. Would anyone deliberately put dirty oil into the crankcase of his car? Not if he valued his car.

The Lord made our bodies for us. Its mechanism is a daily miracle. He has given us instructions for taking care of them. The Word of Wisdom, given in February 1833, at a time when many scientific facts were not known about the detrimental effects of alcohol and tobacco on the body mechanism, specifically advises against the use of strong drinks, which have been interpreted as alcohol, and hot drinks, which have been interpreted as tea and coffee; and against the use of tobacco. Science, only within our own lifetime, has confirmed what was revealed so long ago. As well as warning us about the "dirty oils" that might clog our body mechanism, the Word of Wisdom discusses many positive things that men should do in the care of their physical make-up. These teachings also have been confirmed by science in our day.

Since we know what we should do to keep our body mechanisms running smoothly and faithfully, let us beware of anything that would clog or slow down its functioning.

A Door Closes, a Door Opens

Items Needed

A room with doors in it, to be opened and closed at appropriate times.

Action During Presentation

Open one door representing entrance into mortality (birth), and another door representing exit from life (death).

Suggested Wording for Presentation

Mortality is like a room. We enter through a door—the door called birth; we spend our allotted years of life in mortality in this room called earth. We leave through another door, the door called death. Once these doors are opened, we never use them for a second time.

Mortality can be likened to our sojourn in this room. While we are here, it is our privilege to decorate the room to our own liking and tastes. Of course, we will be held responsible for what we do, how we decorate, just as an earthly landlord may not like the way we decorate his property. And we will have to live with the accumulations we bring into our lives, whether they are uplifting or degrading. Fortunately, we can clean and redecorate our room of mortality as our tastes and preferences grow and progress.

Each day of mortality also has many doors that open and close in it. Alfred, Lord Tennyson wrote in his Locksley Hall, "Every door . . . opens but to golden keys." What are the golden keys that open doors to us? How do we obtain them? Where do we learn to use them? How many of us carry the proper golden keys to activate the right opportunity at the right time?

One of the most popular sentences concerning doors comes from the Spanish writer Cervantes who said in his *Don Quixote*, Book 1, Chapter 21:

"When one door is shut, another opens."

How much happier our lives would sometimes be if only we looked toward the opening door with thrilling anticpation, rather than to the closing one with a twinge of regret?

Each Member Makes the Church

Items Needed

A number of pieces of white paper (perhaps 8x11.)

Action During Presentation

Show whole piece of white paper as representing the whole action of the Church. Show other pieces as each individual's action in the Church. You may need at some times to superimpose one individual piece over the piece representing the whole church.

Suggested Wording for Presentation

For a moment, let us consider this piece of paper as the Church—whole and complete in its organization for the good of man. Though its physical appearance is whole and complete, it is a blank piece of paper. Spiritually its strength is drawn from the contributions of faith and integrity and obedience and spiritual qualities of its members. Thus each ward or stake draws its spirit from its members. In this way each member helps to make the Church and will some time answer for what he does or does not do.

Let us consider this piece of paper as the Church as Joe sees it. It is whole and complete in structure. But, what if Joe thinks that keeping the Sabbath day holy is not always necessary. That part of the Church structure Joe discards. (tear a piece away.) This second piece of paper is the Church as Bill sees it. Bill thinks it is a fine full way of life.

However, once a year Bill attends a New Year's Eve party, and when drinks are passed around, he shares them. There goes a corner of Bill's Church. (tear off a piece.) Superimpose Bill's image of the Church and Joe's image of the Church over the structure of the Church as it should be and there are weaknesses in the whole pattern.

The Church is wonderful. It exists to make better men and women here and to help them towards eternal salvation. But for each individual member this church is largely what we make it.

If, in its perfect organization, it operates in your life, it will function wholly and completely as this whole and complete piece of paper.

Every Person Carries Keys

Items Needed

A ring of keys—large keys, small ones, all shapes and sizes.

Action During Presentation

Indicate various keys as areas of activity and blessings are discussed.

Suggested Wording for Presentation

Every person who dies (and everyone will die) carries with him some keys—evidencing the right to certain blessings he has earned for the things he has done on earth. A small key, like this one, may have been earned through kindness in helping an elderly person across the street, for instance. (It may be more important than that—it may have been the only kindness given to that elderly person in a very long time.) The key may have received its high polish through much use, through many kindnesses given.

There are keys that all will wish to carry. The key of baptism is one—baptism by authority, the only entrance into the Kingdom of God. What will happen to those who have not received this key?

There are other keys that will be necessary—those keys that indicate good works and obedience to law here upon the earth. Many will carry a nearly complete set. Others will be lacking some of the important ones.

How do those persons feel, who having left the earth, find they do not have the necessary keys, or the desired keys, or enough keys for full happiness, or any right keys at all?

In speaking of the authority in the Church, Jesus promised:

"And I will give unto thee the keys of the kingdom of heaven; and whatsoever thou shalt bind on earth shall be bound in heaven; and whatsoever thou shalt loose on earth shall be loosed in heaven." (Matt. 16:19.)

That is the kind of keys most desired—with the individual keys kept bright through good use and activity.

Example Is . . .

Items Needed

A gingerbread boy, a ceramic figurine—something that has been formed, baked in a mold and hardened.

Action During Presentation

Show the outlines formed, the hardness and set of the finished product.

Suggested Wording for Presentation

Just a short time ago this figurine, this gingerbread boy, was soft and pliable. It was shaped and formed and molded. Now, short of destruction, it defies change.

"To every thing there is a season, and a time to every purpose under the heaven:" say the scriptures (Ecc. 3:1.) There is a season for forming and molding, and time for completion and setting. One of the many things that must be accomplished according to the season and the time is providing for the training of our children.

Example, although not the only teacher, is a good teacher. The writer of the Biblical Proverbs enters the field of child-rearing with these words: "Train up a child in the way he should go; and when he is old, he will not depart from it." (Prov. 22:6.)

In this Dispensation the Lord has admonished:

". . . inasmuch as parents have children in Zion, or in any of her stakes, . . . that teach them not to understand the

24

doctrine of repentance, faith in Christ, the Son of the living God, and of baptism and the gift of the Holy Ghost by the laying on of the hands, when eight years old, the sin be upon the heads of the parents." (D&C 68:25.)

To this people President David O. McKay has said: "No other success can compensate for failure in the home." (Opening General Conference address, April 1964.)

The family is an eternal unit of the Church, with the parents as its presidency. It is easier to teach children, to form their attitudes and characters, when they are young and eager; but no one ever grows beyond the time when he can no longer learn. The Lord desires family units, with parents who have properly taught their children, to be with Him always.

Except a Corn of Wheat

Items Needed

A kernel of wheat, or a packet of seeds, a container of soil for planting the seed.

Action During Presentation

Show seeds; plant a seed or more in the soil.

Suggested Wording for Presentation

Jesus said, "Verily, verily, I say unto you, Except a corn of wheat fall into the ground and die, it abideth alone; but if it die, it bringeth forth much fruit."

The stores have blossomed out with pretty packets of seeds, tempting the shopper to buy them. If you yielded to the temptation and bought the seeds and took them home, and put them on the shelf nothing would ever come of them. And you would have lost your money. But if you take the seeds out of the packets, place them in the prepared ground, and lovingly care for them, they will produce after their kind—flowers or vegetables.

Two lessons are taught in the burial of the seeds. The dry, uninteresting seeds must die before the flower lives. The kernel must be lost in the production of the beautiful fruit. Jesus taught: "He that loveth his life shall lose it; and he that hateth his life in this world shall keep it unto life eternal." Like the seed he who loses his life in bringing forth beauty of good works, he who giveth his life for the greater good shall know the greater life—eternal life.

In practicing what he preached, Jesus was willing to lay down his own life for others. He said, "And I, if I be lifted up from the earth, shall draw all men unto me." The record added this comment, "This he said signifying what death he should die."

Jesus did not have to die like the rest of us, for John says, "In him was life . . ." And Jesus said of himself: "For as the Father hath life in himself, so hath he given to the Son to have life in himself." Then he added: "Therefore, doth my Father love me, because I lay down my life, that I might take it up again. No man taketh it from me, but I lay it down of myself; I have power to lay it down and I have power to take it again."

The dry uninteresting seeds, to all appearances dead, when planted in good soil spring forth as the result of the life that is within them. So in this life, as we lose our lives in service to our fellowmen, we bring forth beauty and good works; and as we lay down our lives in death, we come forth to a greater life and resurrection because of Jesus. The scriptures say: "Jesus said unto her, I am the resurrection, and the life; he that believeth in me, though he were dead, yet shall he live; and whosoever liveth and believeth in me shall never die."

Fit the Task at Hand

Items Needed

A very large hammer and a small tack; a small monkey wrench and a section of very large pipe.

Action During Presentation

Use exaggerated action to show the ineffectiveness of finding the small tack with the large hammer, or using the small wrench on the large pipe.

Suggested Wording During Presentation

There are many ways of doing the tasks we are called on to do. There are many helpful and effective tools provided for us to do certain tasks.

Among the steps of preparation for any task a first necessary step would be to know what tool would most effectively help us do our work, what need of implement we have to get the task done, and which size, style, type, or kind best suits our purpose. (Demonstrate the ineffectiveness of the wrong tool.) The implications here are obvious: the tool must fit the task at hand.

On the spiritual side, the lessons to be presented should be shaped and worded, ideally coordinate to the capacities and the needs of those who are to receive the most from the presentation. The method of presentation, the visual aids, the reference books used, the examples and analogies selected are tools to aid the presentation of any lesson. The tools of teaching are many and varied. For the most successful teaching, fit the tool you use or choose to the task.

From Living Material

Item Needed

A pearl.

Action During Presentation

Show the pearl.

Suggested Wording for Presentation

Referring to the value of testimonies, many speakers quote the words of the Savior, given in the Sermon on the Mount:

"Give not that which is holy unto the dogs, neither cast ye your pearls before swine, lest they trample them under their feet, and turn again and rend you." (Matt. 7:6.)

A pearl, like a testimony, is made from living material. If it is not worn, but tenderly put away, hidden, unused, a pearl, like a testimony, soon loses its lustre and its value.

A pearl finds birth as something new and strange enters the life of an oyster. It may be fought against, resisted, momentarily, but if it persists, the pearl begins to grow and grow day by day throughout the life of the oyster.

It is so with a testimony—some of the greatest ones have been resisted, fought against in the beginning, as was the testimony of Saul, who became the Apostle Paul of the New Testament, and Alma the Younger, the church leader and great judge of the Book of Mormon.

Matthew records that one day "went Jesus out of the house, and sat by the sea side." It was a marvelous day for the telling of parables, one of which was:

"Again, the kingdom of heaven is like unto a merchant man, seeking goodly pearls;

"Who, when he had found one pearl of great price, went and sold all that he had, and bought it." (Matt. 13:45-46.)

Who among us would not give all that he had for a testimony? Such is the value of a testimony. It is beyond price. Guard it well.

Found Not Wanting

Items Needed

A ruler, measuring cup, measuring spoon, eyedropper, etc.

Action During Presentation

Hold up to class, and demonstrate in pantomime the use of each object.

Suggested Wording for Presentation

I have with me some instruments for measuring. Will you share with me your ideas as to how each one can be used. For instance, a ruler is used to measure lengths, breadths, spaces, heights. A cup is used often in cooking, in preparing foods in the kitchen. A measuring spoon brings to mind medicines given children and the lingering taste of the 'cough' medicine. An eyedropper measuring minute drops of help in many forms. (Invite class to participate.)

There is a scriptural phrase about being weighed and found not wanting. Medicines, foods, heights, distances can be measured and weighed and seldom are found wanting.

How would you measure a person. What would be the measuring instrument to be used with a man or a woman?

Perhaps one very good indicator would be: how close are we living in accordance with the gospel principles? Perhaps receiving a temple recommend is one of the measuring rods that the Lord uses to size up the worth of a man.

From Our Own Small Vantage Point

Items Needed

Magnifying glass or a projector with appropriate picture.

Action During Presentation

Show the picture on the slide projector, with the projector out of focus; or invite the group to see one enlarged word through the magnifying glass.

Suggested Wording for Presentation

When we see the picture through the glass of the projector, and that projector is out of focus, sometimes we see the picture blurred or distorted. This is sometimes as we see the work of the Lord from our own small vantage point. We seldom see the complete picture fully in focus to our way of thinking. Sometime, it has been promised, the complete picture, fully in focus, will be seen and understood.

The one word, too, enlarged from a single page, does not bring the full meaning.

The Apostle Paul had something to say on the subject of understanding some of the great things of the Kingdom. In his first letter to the Saints of Corinth he penned in the section which has been called the New Testament Psalm on Love:

"For now we see through a glass, darkly; but then face to face; now I know in part; but then shall I know even as also I am known." (I Cor. 13:12.)

God Give Us Men

Items Needed

A piece of paper cut in the shape of a man.

Action During Presentation

As discussion proceeds, show the flimsy character of the paper, that it does not stand upright, or have movement of its own.

Suggested Wording for Presentation

Yes, this is a paper man. It has no backbone; it does not think; it has not a steady or ready hand to help.

This is not the kind of man we need today.

President Heber J. Grant, seventh President of the Church, used to quote to the Church a poem that he learned as a young man. The philosophy in it is as good today as it was the day J. G. Holland penned it many years ago:

"God give us men. A time like this demands
Strong minds, great hearts, true faith and ready hands.
Men whom the lust of office does not kill!
Men whom the spoils of office cannot buy;
Men who possess opinions and a will;
Men who have honor, men who will not lie;
Men who can stand before a demagogue
And damn his treacherous flatteries without winking.
Tall men, sun-crowned, who live above the fog
In public duty and in private thinking.

For while the rabble with their thumb-worn creeds,
Their large professions and their little deeds,
Mingle in selfish strife—lo! Freedom weeps;
Wrong rules the land; and waiting Justice sleeps."

God give us men? Let us be such men, and give ourselves to God.

God Gives Us Talents

Items Needed

Two similar articles of clothing: one moth-eaten, but otherwise apparently unused; the other, well-worn and still valued.

Action During Presentation

Show the two articles of clothing, pointing out the difference.

Suggested Wording for Presentation

Here was a once highly-prized gift. It was prized so highly that it was not placed in immediate use, but was hidden away, waiting for the right occasion to use it. When that occasion came, it was found that the once beautiful and valued item had been destroyed by moths.

But here is a second gift. It was well used and fully valued from the first. It is now frayed, perhaps beyond any hope of repairs, but the owner still finds a friendliness and a warmth in it whenever he sees it, contrasted with the revolting thoughts of seeing what the moths have done with the first gift.

Some lives are a little like the first item. God gives us our talents, but we often do not appreciate their true worth and put off using them until just the right occasion. Then, when it is too late it is found that what was held as precious has vanished.

One of the parables that the Christ told as he walked among men concerns a man traveling in a far country who distributed goods to his servants. One received five talents, another two, and another one. Later as an accounting was made, the servants who had the five and two showed an increase, but the one possessing one had hidden his talent away. (Matt. 25:14-30.)

Let's shape our lives and our talents as they were intended to be used.

How Indispensible Are You?

Items Needed

A wide-mouth glass jar, filled with water.

Action During Presentation

First action, put finger in water, pull it out, as conversation describes the consequences; second action, put fist in bottle and splash around before pulling it out.

Suggested Wording for Presentation

How indispensible are you? How indispensible am I? For a moment let's call this jar of water the sea of humanity, and this little finger will represent me. Let's see how big a hole is left if the finger is suddenly pulled out of the water. Not a very big hole, is it?

Let's try the experiment with a much "bigger person," with one more important to the world, the sea of humanity. Put entire hand, including wrist in the bottle. And let's try splashing the sea of humanity around to let it know that we are here before we withdraw it. How big a hole does it leave when we withdraw the entire hand? Not much, to be sure.

It would seem that we are not indispensible, that we do not leave much of an impression when we withdraw. Of course, there may be a way to permanently leave a depression in this water when we leave it. That would be to freeze all activity and make it ice. But if we do that, we would certainly take a chance of freezing ourselves in and we may even destroy the whole thing as we attempt to turn the water into ice.

Conversion Spots

Items Needed

A picture of a leopard

Action During Presentation

Show the picture; if possible cover some of the spots with colored paper to obliterate them, as the dialogue discusses that.

Suggested Wording for Presentation

The dictionary defines the leopard as: "A large and ferocious spotted cat of southern Asia and Africa. Its color is tawny with black spots."

You have seen the leopard in a circus, at the zoo, or in pictures such as these. He is not a creature that you would expect to see in Church very often. (It seems that lambs have traditionally better dispositions for church literature illustration.) But today, let's consider the leopard—our spotted friend.

Why? Because we once heard of a person who wasn't fully converted. According to his own description he was converted "just in spots." And we thought of the leopard.

The leopard would really look sick if you removed his spots. In fact, it has been said that "a leopard cannot lose his spots." And after all, we are not interested in the leopard; we are interested in the man.

A man has within him the power to change. We are not interested in having him lose the "spots of conversion" that he now has. We are more interested in helping him obtain a "complete conversion" rather than just being converted in spots.

If the man wishes to get his conversion spots so close together that they are now no longer spots but constant in their view, what should he do? The answer is in "Interest and Activity." Get interested and get active—wholly and completely.

I Don't Have My Notes

Items Needed

A few of the usual things carried in a pocket or purse, including an American fifty-cent piece or silver dollar. An extra word of caution: our meetings are a place for reverence. Handle this one so as to not disturb that spirit.

Action During Presentation

Take out items from purse as the talking indicates. Conclude with coin.

Suggested Wording for Presentation

"I had some notes for this address here some place. There is yesterday's grocery list, and the light bill to be paid tomorrow, and a prescription that I should have had filled last week, and here is a letter I forgot to mail.

"I don't seem to have my notes. . . . Say, this coin has a good subject for a short address upon it: 'In God We Trust.' Have you ever thought about that?"

Then go on and develop the theme, "In God We Trust," from a personal or national point of view.

The "I" Is Important

Items Needed

A photograph or two of the group to whom you speak, that was taken on a previous occasion.

Action During Presentation

Pass the photograph or photographs among the members.

Suggested Wording for Presentation

After each one has seen the picture, we can discuss it for a moment.

What were you looking for in the picture? Why, yourself, of course. Didn't you check to see if your eyes were closed, whether the smile was good, and a half-hundred other things about yourself in the photograph.

The "I" is important to the individual. Rare indeed is he who does not think "I" first.

The individual is tremendously important in the gospel, too. The gospel is working basically with individuals. They may participate in some things as groups—and they certainly do, but it is the individual and his testimony that counts. The gospel means an individual conversion, an individual baptism, an individual activity all leading to individual salvation. Along the way individuals make families and all work toward the common goal.

The "I" in "Individual" is very important.

"I Take My Ring From My Finger . . ."

Item Needed

A finger ring (preferably the wedding band type.)

Action During Presentation

As you proceed with discussion, show ring with the words, "I take my ring, etc."

Suggested Wording for Presentation

"Man was also in the beginning with God. Intelligence, or the light of truth, was not created or made, neither indeed can be." (D&C 93:29.)

That revelation was given at Kirtland, Ohio, May 6, 1833. Almost eleven years later, April 7, 1844, the Prophet Joseph Smith spoke before about twenty thousand Saints assembled at Nauvoo, Illinois, for the general conference. There he said:

"I am dwelling on the immortality of the spirit of man. Is it logical to say that the intelligence of spirits is immortal, and yet that it has a beginning? The intelligence of spirits had no beginning, neither will it have an end. That is good logic. That which has a beginning may have an end. There never was a time when there were not spirits; for they are co-equal (co-eternal) with our Father in Heaven.

"I want to reason more on the spirit of man; for I am dwelling on the body and spirit of man—on the subject of the dead. I take my ring from my finger and liken it unto the mind of man—the immortal part, because it had no beginning. Suppose you cut it in two; then it has a beginning and an end, but join it again, and it continues one eternal round. So with the spirit of man. As the Lord liveth, if it had a beginning, it will have an end. All the fools and learned wise men from the beginning of creation, who say that the spirit of man had a beginning, prove that it must have an end; and if that doctrine is true, then the doctrine of annihilation would be true." * (*Documentary History of the Church 6:311.*)

---

*About a month before, King Follett, a trusted Elder, had died, "by the accidental breaking of a rope, and the falling of a bucket of rock upon him, while engaged in walling up a well, and the men above were in the act of lowering the rock to him." Although an appropriate funeral was held, the subject of man's existence was still on the Prophet's mind as he arose to speak that Sabbath conference afternoon. His sermon has come to be known as the "King Follett Discourse."

If a Page Is Missing

Items Needed

A book or magazine no longer of value that can be torn; mending tape.

Action During Presentation

Tear out the page from the magazine when the dialogue intends for this action, and repair the book when indicated.

Suggested Wording for Presentation

Someone has likened the family to a book; each page and each family member adds something. If a page is missing, or if a family member removes himself, or tears himself away like this, of course that book or that family is no longer complete, no longer has its full value of potentials.

Then, sometimes after many long years there is repentance, a change of heart, a desire to rejoin, and come back. That way is never the easiest thing to do, it is said. But it can be accomplished, just as we can replace this page in the book with a piece of mending tape.

The illustration is admittedly crude, but there are professional bookbinders who can and do restore pages of books to their original place; in fact, they can restore old and precious books so that for all intents and purposes they do not appear new; they are new.

Sincere hearts who are willing to make a correction in their lives also find the blue print to repentance well marked.

I Wonder How Great

Item Needed

Toy sword (wood or heavy cardboard).

Action During Presentation

Show toy while talking; read verse from blade.

Suggested Wording for Presentation

This sword does not represent Laban's sword that Nephi carried with him to the New World (1 Nephi chapter 4.); or the sword with which the Apostle Peter cut off Malchus' ear, to have the Christ immediately restore it (John 18:10-11); (Luke 22:50-51); or even one of the many swords that will be beaten into plowshares as peace comes into the world at the Millennium (Isaiah 2:4.)

It is intended to represent a two-edged sword that cuts either way. The way depends on how firm and active and strong the testimony is of the one who holds it in his hand. For an active member it cuts one way, and for one not so active it will cut the other.

According to the books that record history and legend the knights of old sometimes had phrases engraved upon the blades of their swords. This is such a sword, because on its blade is written:

> "I wonder how great
> This Church would be
> If all the members
> Were just like me."

If You Only See

Item Needed

A light bright enough to create a shadow.

Action During Presentation

Demonstrate how you can cast your shadow to various parts of the room. The position you are in controls the shadow. Call attention to that fact that you, yourself, and only you, control your shadow.

Suggested Wording During Presentation

We have a wonderful Church that has given us eternal principles we should apply in the living of our daily lives. Like the shadow, we, and only we, control just how many of those principles of the gospel become a part of our very beings. We must all strive to be on our way to perfection. Perfection, to us, is a road rather than a destination.

But there have been people who have applied the principles of the gospel to their lives in such a way that—well, you know the story of the residents of the city of Enoch, and the story of the translated prophets, Moses and Elijah, and other stories. These people certainly had the ability to live the eternal laws of the gospel in such a way that they received these blessings.

Notice how our position in the light controls our shadow. See how we can control the placement of our shadow. We are in complete control here. For a moment, think of the light here as the light of the gospel. That light is constant. We have been creating our shadows by moving around, not by moving the light. The choice and the activity have always been ours. And we can move in such a way as to completely block the light from view. Many do that to the gospel light as well. So . . .

> "If you only see your shadow
> Remember what we say—
> The gospel light is always shining
> But you're sometimes in the way."

The Important Thing

Items Needed

A large dishpan. An assortment of various kinds and shapes of bottles. Colored water.

Action During Presentation

Place the open empty bottles in the dishpan. Pour the colored liquid into the bottles, some full and some part way. The dishpan will collect the excess.

Suggested Wording for Presentation

The Lord has use for everyone, no matter what his capacity for religion is. Some people differ as these bottles differ in their capacity to hold and receive the gospel truths. (Pour water) Some souls are large enough to comprehend the greatness of the gospel; other smaller persons receive all that they can; some who are large enough for great comprehension receive only small portions. Others who are small in size seem to bubble over with love and enthusiasm in their containment of the gospel.

If you were a musician you might play a hymn using these filled and partially filled bottles that range from low reception to completely overflowing, that are large or small in size.

(At this point you have arranged for someone to come in and play the organ, demonstrating first how the large pipes, if it is a pipe organ, make the tune sound when they are played alone, and how the small pipes sound when they are played alone, then how well they sound when they are played together in a well known and much-beloved hymn.)

The important thing is not necessarily the capacity of these bottles for the colored water, or the size of the pipes in the organ, but how well they are "tuned." Similarly the important thing with us is how well we are attuned to the work of the Lord.

An Individual Something Like This

Items Needed

From the drugstore some iron sulphate, tannic acid, and oxalic acid. These substances are *poisonous*. Containers appropriate for two of them—a salt shaker, either without a top, or with enlarged holes, and a glass of water.

Action During Presentation

Mix chemicals with water as dialogue indicates.

Suggested Wording for Presentation

Here is a glass of crystal clear water. It can be likened to the friendliness of a good neighborhood. All neighbors are not alike, and sometimes in the hurried existence of today, the second great commandment: "Thou shalt love thy neighbour as thyself. There is none other commandment greater. . . ." (Mark 12:31.) is all but forgotten about.

Now place in the glass of water—the neighborhood— two such people who are hurting each other's feelings. There is one of that type. (Place in the glass a small crystal of iron sulphate, one about the size of a pea.) There's another basically good individual something like this. (Drop about three pinches of tannic acid in the glass. As they mix with the water and with each other the liquid will turn black.)

Jesus once called the people "the salt of the earth." Perhaps these people—this special kind—should get busy in that kind of neighborhood. We have this kind of good neighbor represented in the salt shaker. (Have about a half teaspoonful of oxalic acid in the shaker.) Now see what happens if we mix some of this group into the glass.

(The liquid will immediately clear.)

In Obedience to Law

Item Needed

A color television set

Action During Presentation

Tune the video part of the set so that the signals being received are all wrong—the "reds" are coming in as "greens," etc. Later, correct the tuning.

Suggested Wording for Presentation

Have we done something wrong here? It would indeed be nice to sit quietly and enjoy a good television program, but the reception at this moment here leaves much to be desired. Looking at it for an extended period of time in this condition would not bring satisfaction at all.

Yet, basically, television is one of the good things of life to be enjoyed. In the great counsel given by Father Lehi of the Book of Mormon to his son Jacob, he spoke: ". . . men are, that they might have joy." (2 Nephi 2:25)

This program in its present condition gives no joy.

What is the matter? Is it the fault of the television transmitter? Are faulty signals being sent? Before we make any accusations in that direction, let's investigate and adjust the tuning we have done. There, is that better?

We speak of joy—and joy sometimes is just another way of saying the word, "blessing." A blessing comes in obedience to law. We retuned our television set—it now conforms to the ways of natural law, and we are receiving the picture as it is intended that we should receive it.

Some important items of instruction given by the Prophet Joseph Smith are:

"There is a law, irrevocably decreed in heaven before the foundations of the world, upon which all blessings are predicated—

"And when we obtain any blessing from God, it is by obedience to that law upon which it is predicated." (D&C 130:20-21.)

It All Just Happened

Items Needed

Ten milk bottle caps on which the numerals one to ten have previously been written; a box or other container.

Action During Presentation

Place the ten milk bottle caps in the box. Shake well. Ask a member of the class to take one cap from the box. (Admit that maybe he should be blindfolded to do it right.)

Suggested Wording for Presentation

Now that you have selected one from the ten numbered milk bottle caps, tell us what number is on this one. (The class member gives the number.)

Whatever it is, this person had only one chance in ten of picking number "one" from the box that way. He would have had one chance in 90 to get numbers "one" and "two" in consecutive tries.

And the chances would be one in 3,628,800 to have taken all ten numbers, in consecutive order, from the box.

Of course, the milk bottle caps choice is just a simple problem. But there are those who would tell us that we human beings, who contain millions of cells, happened just that way—that one cell was added to another to build our magnificent bodies. Could it all just happen without any guiding Intelligence behind it? We think not.

Just a Little Sin

Items Needed

A sponge and some colored water in a pan.

Action During Presentation

Place the colored water in the pan. Touch one end of the sponge into the water, carefully.

Suggested Wording for Presentation.

Suppose I want to get just the small corner of this sponge colored in this colored water. Soon, no matter how careful I am, in my desire to get just a little of the sponge wet, the colored water has entered into much of the sponge. It is just that way with those who desire to try just a little sin!

The First of Many Doors

Items Needed

A key and a nearby door.

Action During Presentation

Turn the lock on the door with the key.

Suggested Wording for Presentation

It was the regular baptismal service. The candidates for the ordinance were there, clothed in white. The men holding the Priesthood were there ready to baptize them in the name of the Lord Jesus Christ.

The speaker said: "I have here a key in my hand. It turns the lock on this door. Today someone holding the priesthood will baptize you. He will be opening the lock of a spiritual door for you. But while he holds the key and unlocks the door, you must open that door and advance yourself into the kingdom of the Father!"

Baptism is but the first of many door experiences that will bring us to salvation. Each has a common characteristic. Someone with authority stands with the key, but we must step through the door and advance after the key is used and the door is opened.

A call to teach must precede an individual's teaching an auxiliary class of the Church. A call must precede the entering of missionary service and preaching the gospel.

The Church is rightly an organization of authority and of order.

A Kind of Gun

Item Needed

A "spent" bullet

Action During Presentation

Show the empty bullet, the "spent" bullet, pointing out the markings that identify the gun that fired it.

Suggested Wording for Presentation

There are experts who can examine a bullet like this, and by the markings on it they can identify the very gun that fired the bullet. Every gun leaves a different marking on the bullets it fires.

We wish to speak of a different kind of gun, and a different kind of "gray matter."

The kind of guns are "ideas." The kind of gray matter is the human mind, especially the young and impressionable one. And idea—whether it be an unspoken thought, a conversation with friends, something one sees, or something one reads—marks the mind as it passes through it, just as surely as a bullet is marked as it passes through a gun. Therefore, it behooves us all to let our minds come in contact with only the best that life has to offer.

The Kind of Light You Have

Items Needed

A room temporarily darkened; a flashlight; a light switch.

Action During Presentation

Begin with darkened room; open doors or windows to let in partial light; flash the flashlight for glimpses of light; then turn on the switch to flood the room with light.

Suggested Wording for Presentation

What is the best way to get the darkness out of such a room as this? We could open the doors and a little of the darkness would disappear. Or we could use a flashlight, and a little more of the darkness would disappear, in addition to having the doors open, or we could touch the switch and flood the whole room with light! (Action as indicated.)

Now, sin is called darkness, and scripturally, the gospel is called the light. Those who live the gospel principles do testify that it is the light! But how much of this light are we going to let into our lives?

Are we going to be content by opening a few darkened windows? Or doors? Or by turning on a flashlight? Flashlight is a good word for this light. How many of us know people who seek the gospel light only on Sunday, and seemingly like to live by their own devices the rest of the week?

How many of us are going to flood our lives with the gospel light, as we do this room with light?

Remember the choice is yours—your activity creates the kind of light you have.

We open a door, we turn a flashlight on now and then, or we turn the switch that floods the whole area with the light.

Knowing the Genuine

Items Needed

Some genuine money and poorly drawn counterfeits.

Action During Presentation

Show the genuine money and the poorly drawn counterfeits.

Suggested Wording for Presentation

No one would think about accepting poorly made counterfeits of the real thing. It is the cleverly made counterfeits that sometimes are mistaken for the real. Bankers and law enforcement officers say that it is easy to identify counterfeit money by knowing the genuine item and comparing the two.

The purpose of this discussion is not money but religion. Do you know the scriptures well enough to know if your religious affiliation is true, or is it to be found counterfeit when the test is made?

In speaking to the law and the testimony, the Old Testament Prophet Isaiah recorded:

". . . if they speak not according to this word, it is because there is no light in them." (Isa. 8:20.)

How much light is in your church? In preaching to the people the Apostle Peter foresaw ". . . when the times of refreshing shall come from the presence of the Lord:

"And he shall send Jesus Christ which before was preached unto you:

"Whom the heaven must receive until the times of restitution of all things, which God hath spoken by the mouth of all his holy prophets since the world began." (Acts 3:19-21.)

The Leadership Must Come

Item Needed

An acorn.

Action During Presentation

Show acorn while reading the poem.

Suggested Wording for Presentation

My friends, behold this tiny fruit:
    It seems a wondrous thing,
That, wrapt up in an acorn's shell,
    Should live a forest king.

But plant it in a genial soil,
    And as the years roll round,
Then may you see a hardy plant
    Appear above the ground.

Observe its growth: it rises high;
    Its limbs stretch far and wide;
The acorn has become a tree;
    The tree, the woodland's pride.

And though a boy, I am a Saint,
    And hope to be a man,
To grow in grace and understand
    The Gospel's mighty plan,

To build up temples to the Lord,
    To spread his truths abroad,
And on Mount Zion, when redeemed,
    To stand—*a son of God.*

—Edward S. Shaw

The story of the Old Testament Samuel and his mother, Hannah, is familiar to all. Her most earnest prayers for the great blessing of a son were answered, and in obedience to her part of the promise she brought the very small Samuel to the temple where he was reared in the ways of the priesthood to become a leader in Ancient Israel. (1 Sam. 1, 2.)

Modern Israel, the Church of today, is constantly searching for leadership for the wards and stakes. The leadership must come from a prepared youth. For the most part the homes of today are preparing these youth for their callings of tomorrow.

Let Silence Reign Supreme

Item Needed

A watch with a second hand.

Action During Presentation

A couple of casual and unsuspecting glances at the sweeping second hand of your watch.

Suggested Wording for Presentation

Ask for quiet. Let the silence reign supreme. Then ask, what was that? Yes, it was silence, but it was something more. It was a block of time—fifteen, thirty, fifty-nine seconds long. That much time would be worth a fortune to a television network if sold for advertising purposes. But what could you accomplish with that much time?

Time is about the only thing that is constant. Twenty-four hours a day, not one minute more nor less, is graciously given to each of us.

Some of us have learned to budget our time better than others. What can you do with fifteen, or thirty, or fifty-nine seconds? What would you do with it if you knew that it was your last fifteen, thirty, or fifty-nine seconds that would be allotted to you here upon the earth?

Jesus once told a parable concerning the uncertainty of time that is left in mortality for a man:

"The ground of a certain rich man brought forth plentifully;

"And he thought within himself, saying, What shall I do, because I have no room where to bestow my fruits?

"And he said, This will I do: I will pull down my barns, and build greater; and there will I bestow all my fruits and my goods.

"And I will say to my soul, Soul, thou hast much goods laid up for many years; take thine ease, eat, drink, and be merry.

"But God said unto him, Thou fool, this night thy soul shall be required of thee; then whose shall these things be, which thou hast provided?

"So is he that layeth up treasure for himself, and is not rich toward God." (Luke 12:16-21.)

Look at the Stem

Items Needed

A very healthy-looking houseplant; scissors or other pruning instrument.

Action During Presentation

This sermon to see is a two-time presentation. In the first class period, cut the stem from the growing plant; put it aside. In the second class period, point out to the class the withered stem when separated from the growing plant.

Suggested Wording for Presentation

Last class period, as you remember, we cut from this healthy growing plant a stem, or branch. Let us look again at the plant. It is probably as healthy and as beautiful as ever. Now, let us look at the stem that was cut from the plant. It is dry and withered. What happened? It was severed from the plant, its source of strength. In being cut off from the plant, it lost its strength and its purpose.

Just so those members who cut themselves off from the growing living Church of our Lord, cut themselves away from their source of strength and faith. This is a plea to keep active in the Church.

Speaking to the apostles, the night of the Last Supper, Jesus said:

"I am the true vine, and my Father is the husbandman.

"Every branch in me that beareth not fruit he taketh

away; and every branch that beareth fruit, he purgeth it, that it may bring more fruit.

"Now, ye are clean, through the word which I have spoken unto you.

"Abide in me, and I in you. As the branch cannot bear fruit of itself, except it abide in the vine; no more can ye, except ye abide in me.

"I am the vine, ye are the branches; He that abideth in me, and I in him, the same bringeth forth much fruit; for without me ye can do nothing.

"If a man abide not in me, he is cast forth as a branch, and is withered; and men gather them, and cast them into the fire, and they are burned.

"If ye abide in me, and my words abide in you, ye shall ask what ye will, and it shall be done unto you.

"Here in is my Father glorified, that ye bear much fruit; so shall ye be my disciples." (John 15:1-8.)

Lost: Many Important Parts

Items Needed

Two copies of the same picture, such as a beautiful seascape cut from a magazine. One copy should be cut in jig-saw puzzle fashion.

Action During Presentation

At the beginning of the discussion show only the copy of the picture that has been cut, with some of its parts cut away. Later when the discussion calls for it, show the other copy of the whole complete picture.

Suggested Wording for Presentation

When Jesus Christ was here in mortality he gave us a wonderful plan of salvation, and there is increasing evidence (discovered by the scientific expeditions of the world) that the ancient prophets knew and understood it.

Many parts of this plan have been lost to the world today, just as some parts of this beautiful picture have been lost. What we see of the picture is beautiful, and the Christian churches on earth today retain many parts of the beautiful gospel plan. At the same time, however, many of the more important parts are lost—as they are missing in the picture.

A falling away was indeed predicted to be followed by a restitution of all things. The restoration was accomplished in the hands of the Prophet Joseph Smith as millions testify.

The plan of salvation, as Jesus gave it to us, is a picture of beauty and one of completeness. (Show the second whole copy of the picture.) It has all the true parts, all the true beauty of the first nowadays incomplete picture, plus many of the parts that could only come to man again by a restoration from heaven.

No Matter Where We Go

Item Needed

A compass.

Action during Presentation

Show and demonstrate the use and working of the compass during talk.

Suggested Wording for Presentation

Several years ago an acquaintance made his first automobile trip from his home in the comparative flatlands of the Midwest to California where he visited a married daughter.

He had read about the mountain passes and was anticipating some firsthand knowledge of them. In preparation for his trip he had a compass installed upon the instrument panel of his new car.

Speaking of the trip for months after it was but a thrilling memory, he often recalled that the "mountain passes were so full of twists that the compass taken along for the purpose was often a full five minutes behind in keeping track of the direction that they were traveling."

A compass may not be a necessity in an automobile, even in the mountain passes of the West, but it is most valuable to not only have one, but an accurate one, for those who "go down to the sea in ships" or who fly high in the blue-vaulted heavens.

The compass here in my hand moves as I move and change my direction around the room. Still the compass really does not move, it registers my moves.

No matter where we go, we should carry with us a compass. Something to keep us always informed as to how well we are doing in relation to what we should be doing in relation to the Church and our participation in its Restored Gospel.

No One Is a Duplicate

Items Needed

Magnifying glass and a flower or a leaf.

Action During Presentation

Show the class the intricate design of the flower or leaf as seen through the magnifying glass. If both a flower and leaf are to be shown, the individuality of each could be pointed out.

Suggested Wording for Presentation

The delicate cells of a plant are small but perfect in form. They all function perfectly for the good of the whole plant. They are, however, all individual. Someone has said that the creations of the Lord are all individual, that no one has ever found one that is an exact duplicate of its neighbor.

Surely, we see the work of the Creator, an Intelligent Being, everywhere if we but look for the evidence.

In the Sermon on the Mount, Jesus called attention to ". . .the lilies of the field, how they grow. . . ."

Then as if citing the power of mortal man, he recalled the wisest man of all and said ". . .even Solomon in all his glory was not arrayed like one of these." (Matt. 6:28-29.)

Mortality May Be Called a Journey

Items Needed

A red, yellow, and green light.

Action During Presentation

Show red, yellow, and green lights at proper time in discussion.

Suggested Wording for Presentation

Mortality is a journey from birth to the grave. Actually the journey began long before time was an element of reckoning. There was a pre-mortal existence as surely as there will be a life for each beyond the grave.

Mortality, as a person walks by faith alone, may be called a journey.

The Church, through giving opportunities for activity, aids in the earthly journey. It has rules to be obeyed if one desires to gain the higher degrees of the kingdoms prepared in heaven.

As in a well-marked highway, the eternal laws governing advancement towards cherished goals sometimes flash yellow warning signals if areas are traversed where such warnings are necessary. A red signal is sometimes used if something is entirely wrong and must be stopped immediately. Of course there are many green signals that permit the flow of life to advance toward the much sought for goal.

Of the Same Mintage

Items Needed

Two coins (pennies, nickels, or dimes) of the same mintage.

Action During Presentation

Show the identities of the coins as being of the same mintage.

Suggested Wording for Presentation

Jesus once comforted His disciples saying:

"I am the way, the truth, and the life; no man cometh unto the Father but by me.

"If ye had known me, ye should have known my Father also, and henceforth ye know him, and have seen him." (John 14:6-7.)

Some have interpreted that as meaning that the Father and the Son are but one Person. They are two separate Identities as the coins are, but they are one in the great purpose of bringing to pass the eternal life of man. (Moses 1:39)

The Apostle Paul adds clarification to the separate identities of the Father and the Son as he begins his testimony to the Hebrews:

"God, who at sundry times and in divers manners spake in time past unto the fathers by the prophets,

"Hath in these last days spoken unto us by his Son, whom he hath appointed heir of all things, by whom also he made the worlds;

"Who being the brightness of his glory, and the express image of his person, and upholding all things by the word of his power, when he had by himself purged our sins, sat down on the right hand of the Majesty on high." (Hebrews 1:1-3.)

One Deed or Act Can Be Broken

Item Needed

Some easily broken thread or string.

Action During Presentation

Demonstrate how easily one piece of thread or string is broken. Then show how difficult, next to impossible, it is to break the thread or string once it is braided so that it puts forth "group resistance."

Wording Suggested for Presentation

We can easily demonstrate how one single piece of thread or string can be broken. (Invite members to participate in demonstration.) But we find it more difficult, next to impossible, to break the string or the thread once it is braided so that it puts forth "group resistance."

Some thoughts come to mind in continuance of this illustration: First, how one deed or act can be broken, as contrasted to how difficult it is to break the combined force of many deeds or acts, in other words, a habit. And habits can as easily be good habits as bad habits.

Second, how much more difficult it is to break the team or cooperative spirit, while the individual spirit can more easily be broken. The cables that support the great suspension bridges of the world are but many small wires twisted together for that purpose.

Ecclesiastes, that wise old preacher, counseled that "Two are better than one; because they have a good reward for their labour.

"For if they fall, the one will lift up his fellow; but woe to him that is alone when he falleth; for he hath not another to help him up." (Ecc. 4:9-10)

Jesus prayed that his disciples might be one. (John 17: 21.)

In our meetings we often sing "The World Has Need of Willing Men" by Will L. Thompson. The refrain is:

"Put your shoulder to the wheel; push along;

Do your duty with a heart full of song;

We all have work; let no man shirk;

Put your shoulder to the wheel."

One Straw Can Start a Whirlpool

Items Needed

Wheat or broom straw, and a container of water.

Action During Presentation

As conversation indicates fill container with water, start the straw in circular motion until all the water is moving in one whirlpool.

Suggested Wording for Presentation

Elder Karl G. Maeser, who did so much in placing what has become Brigham Young University on a solid footing, and who was a power for education in pioneer Utah, used to say that one straw could start a whirlpool and then proceed to demonstrate it. To illustrate his point, he would fill a container with water, and then place a straw in the water, moving the straw in a circular motion until all the water in the container was moving in one whirlpool.

In the travels of Ancient Israel there are recorded incidents where but one was the prime moving force toward accomplishment. Moses voiced the question: "How should one chase a thousand, and two put ten thousand to flight except their Rock had sold them, and the Lord had shut them up?" (Deut. 32:30.)

His successor, Joshua, says: "One man of you shall chase a thousand for the Lord your God, he it is that fighteth for you, and he hath promised you." (Joshua 23:10.)

In another place: "And five of you shall chase an hundred, and an hundred of you shall put ten thousand to flight. . . ." (Lev. 26:8.)

Yes, one small straw can start a whirlpool—but it is within that one small straw to direct the kind of whirlpool to be started.

The Opportunity May Be Gone

Items Needed

A picture cut up in jigsaw-puzzle fashion

Action During Presentation

As discussion centers on organizing material, put the cut pieces of the puzzle in proper sequence so the picture is complete.

Suggested Wording for Presentation

Here are all the parts of a lesson presentation. But it is of little consequence as long as it remains disjointed. It will only speak effectively when it is given in the manner that the lesson was intended to speak, when it is fully organized. It is the responsibility of the teacher or the missionary to organize the material so that the patterns form a related whole, so that each truth falls into place to achieve and complete the lesson goal. (show complete picture)

Many of us are prone to present material in an attitude of finality. If you don't get it now, the opportunity for you is gone. Sometimes one vital part is lost or clouded. Let's try a little harder never to close the door so completely that no opportunity is ours to present another discussion. Remember the Lord has said:

"Remember the worth of souls is great in the sight of God. . . . .

"And if it so be that you should labor all your days

in crying repentance unto this people, and bring, save it be one soul unto me, how great shall be your joy with him in the kingdom of my Father!

"And now, if your joy will be great with one soul that you have brought unto me into the kingdom of my Father, how great will be your joy if you should bring many souls unto me!

"Behold, you have my gospel before you, and my rock, and my salvation." (D&C 18:10, 15-17.)

No One Has Ever Been Promised

Items Needed

Previously prepared papers written upon with invisible ink, the kind that becomes visible when heat is applied. Perhaps it is possible to make this presentation in a kitchen where a stove is available.

Action During Presentation

Apply the paper with message written on it in invisible ink to heat.

Suggested Wording For Presentation

No one has ever been promised that the good life would be without adversity. It is sometimes during the periods of adversity and strain that we can see more distinctly the path ahead which in the wisdom of God we should follow.

The papers here appear to be perfectly blank. But heat, to the paper at least, is a form of adversity. Applying the paper to the heat, the previously written message appears on the apparently blank paper.

The message could be any of the following, or others:

"The Lord is my shepherd; I shall not want.

"He maketh me to lie down in green pastures; he leadeth me beside the still waters.

"He restoreth my soul; he leadeth me in the paths of righteousness for his name's sake. . ." (Psalms 23:1-3.)

Signs of the Times

Items Needed

Some pictures of the freeway traffic signs.

Action During Presentation

Show the pictures as discussion proceeds

Suggested Wording for Presentation

These are indeed the "signs of the times." At the highway speeds traveled on the freeways these signs must be instantly recognized for what they are, and obeyed. Otherwise, there may be only disaster and regret.

Not only must these signs be recognized close at hand, but they must be recognized as we see them far down the highway. There are times too at that distance when the urgent message for us seems to be written on a sign the size of a postage stamp.

If we want to survive we learn to read these signs and apply our knowledge to what they inform us.

But as we travel down life's highways, as we are active in our church duties, how many of us recognize the signs that God has placed perhaps only for us. Most of them can be placed under the great heading of "Follow Counsel."

If we recognize such spiritual markers in our mortal lives, then there is little danger of going amiss as we approach that great goal of "Life Eternal."

Someone Has Taken the Effort

Items Needed

Rocks, a gem stone that has not been polished, and one that has.

Action During Presentation

Demonstrate the difference in the polished and unpolished rock.

Suggested Wording for Presentation

This is a rock. Perhaps we all know where there is a mountain full of such rocks. This rock has some value or no one would go to the effort of bringing it here.

Here is something else. Yes, it is the same rock structure. But someone has taken time and effort to polish it and care for it until it no longer looks like just a rock, but is a beautiful gem stone.

The world is full of members of the human family. Estimates are something like three billion souls. Abraham was given the promise that his posterity would become as numerous as the sands of the sea.

Statistics tend to hide their own possibilities in their own enormity, but when you can see men, not numbers, but men who are willing to submit to a polishing, a preparation for the greater possibilities within them, then you see men who become gem-like in the progress of the world.

That's What Sin Does

Items Needed

A fountain pen using "wet" ink (not a "ball point"); glass of water.

Action During Presentation

Drop a bit of ink into the glass of water.

Suggested Wording for Presentation

Often President David O. McKay, when addressing an audience made up predominantly of young people, will take a glass of water and ask his audience what it is, what it is good for, and comment generally on how pure it looks in the drinking glass.

Then he will take his fountain pen and let one drop of ink fall from the pen into the glass of water. Again, he asks about its present purity, and wonders if any of the young audience would like to drink it. Finally he calls attention to the cloudiness of water and says:

"That's what sin does to your life!"

Something About a Countenance

Item Needed

A prism.

Action During Presentation

Using the prism, show that the light in the room, although it appears to be white, is really a series of bands of color: red, orange, yellow, green, blue, indigo, and violet.

Suggested Wording for Presentation

It has always been said, and many of us can testify, that there is something about the countenance of those who sincerely live the gospel that makes them different from the crowd, and makes it possible for strangers to recognize them in the crowd.

Someone once said that the gospel was a full-course meal in which we were all required to partake of every course, but that many of us seemingly prefer, by our actions at least, to try to partake of the gospel on the cafeteria basis. We would prefer to give ourselves a greater helping of one part of the gospel plan, and pass up another part of the plan entirely.

We need the light of the gospel in all of our activities.

Jesus said of himself as he walked in mortality: "I am the light of the world; he that followeth me shall not walk in darkness, but shall have the light of life." (John 8:12.)

In modern scriptures the Christ is described as: "The

light and the Redeemer of the world, the Spirit of truth, who came into the world, because the world was made by him, and in him was the life of men and the light of men." (D&C 93:9.)

The prism breaks down the white light into various bands of color and physicists show that if the red, or the orange, or any other of the colored bands are removed, the light is not as white as before.

Just as the white light needs all its bands of color from red through violet, so our lives, to be most effective, need to have the entire gospel plan functioning.

In writing to the Ephesians the Apostle Paul admonished:

"Wherefore take unto you the whole armour of God, that ye may be able to withstand in the evil day, and having done all, to stand." (Eph. 6:13.)

He sent the theme to the Romans:

"The night is far spent, the day is at hand; let us therefore cast off works of darkness, and let us put on the armour of light." (Romans 13:12.)

Peter, the Chief Apostle, penned:

". . . giving all diligence, add to your faith virtue; and to your virtue, knowledge;

"And to knowledge temperance; and to temperance patience; and to your patience godliness;

"And to your godliness brotherly kindness; and to brotherly kindness charity.

"For if these things be in you, and abound, they make you that ye shall neither be barren nor unfruitful in the knowledge of our Lord Jesus Christ." (2 Peter 1:5-8.)

The Textbooks of Religion

Items Needed

Copies of the four standard works of the Church: the Bible, the Book of Mormon, the Doctrine and Covenants, and the Pearl of Great Price.

Action During Presentation

At the time of discussion in the presentation, show the pages of the books of scripture, thumbing through rapidly to indicate how many pages in each book.

Suggested Wording for Presentation

A man, well into middle age, once said that he felt he had only ten years of life left, and if those ten years went by as fast as the last ten he was afraid for his future. The thought was upsetting him because he felt he was not prepared for his future. He said he knew nothing about religion, which is the doorway to the eternal future.

This man was well educated for the affairs of his next ten years. He was a college graduate in his field of business. He need not have had fears, for if he had spent as much time and effort mastering the textbooks of religion as he once had the textbooks of college life, he would have little to fear concerning his future.

The textbooks of religion: the Bible—the page count almost always differs with each Bible opened. It is roughly one thousand pages of small-sized printing in that book of scripture. The Book of Mormon is 522 pages, the Doctrine and Covenants, 256 pages, and the Pearl of Great Price, 60 pages. Something less that a total of two thousand pages of scripture.

But what had been required of him at college? Surely, he had had to comprehend that much text to successfully matriculate one year at college.

The textbooks of religion are vital; but there is another side, just as there is another side of college life. In religion that other side is activity. We will be judged not only on how much we know of this thing called religion, but on just how well we practice it.

The Timeless Truths

Items Needed

Some bi-lingual neighbors.

Action During Presentation

Have some of the foreign-speaking converts, or members of your ward who speak a foreign language, come in to your class and teach the class members phrases or words of the native language and the proper pronunciation and intonations, without giving the meaning.

Suggested Wording for Presentation

Now that we have learned how to pronounce these foreign (to us) words, let's speak briefly to the person on our right or left in this new tongue. Do you know what you are saying? Perhaps you are merely saying the timeless greeting, "Hello." "Welcome." "How are you?" Perhaps we are saying words just as true that have not such simple meanings.

It is well often to recall that many scientists of the world are actually doing the same thing. Without knowing it, many of them are discovering and restating some of the Lord's timeless truths of the gospel.

Archeologists, for instance, are doing much to prove the existence of a high culture of civilization in areas of the New World that have been long known by the Church to be Book of Mormon lands. New discoveries in the Holy

Land do much to confirm what our Church has preached for over a century.

Medical science has about confirmed the broad principles contained in the Word of Wisdom.

With these thoughts in mind, let us have our foreign teachers tell us what they have taught us to say. As well as "Hello." and "How are you?" they may have said, "Great and marvelous are the ways of the Lord," or the first Article of Faith: "We believe in God, the Eternal Father, and in His Son, Jesus Christ, and in the Holy Ghost."

A Tonic Pill?

Items Needed

A number of prescription pill bottles. Empty capsules. Prescription labels.

Action During Presentation

Show capsules and bottles, with genealogy prescription, to class.

Suggested Wording for Presentation

In today's modern world we take tonic pills for many ailments—for drowsiness, for sleeplessness, for underweight; for overweight; we take pep pills; we take tranquilizers. There is a tonic pill for almost everything.

One ward genealogy committee tried administering a tonic pill also, in an effort to breathe new life into their ward. With the help of a friendly pharmacist, "pill bottles" were distributed to all members of their ward. The label on the bottle read:

"Prescription No. 1   Dr. Tracy Ancestors

"Mr. and Mrs. _____Ward

"Beginning 0/0/00 (date), take at 7:15 p.m. each Monday for 14 weeks."

Inside the bottle were a number of capsules. Inside the capsules were small papers with such phrases as the following typed neatly.

"Enjoy guest speakers (your friends) and make new ones . . . field trips and a great feeling of accomplishment . . . call (phone number.)

They Do Not Mix

Items Needed

Water, vegetable oil (colored if possible), glass bottle with lid.

Action During Presentation

Pour the water into the bottle; then the oil. Shake the bottle.

Suggested Wording for Presentation

You notice we have poured the water into the bottle; then the oil on top of it. Next, we must shake the bottle well.

How long does it take the water and the oil to separate again? Shake the bottle well again, thoroughly mixing the contents. See that the water and the oil quietly separate again as the bottle is put down.

It is a proven scientific fact that water and oil do not mix.

It is just as much a fact that true prayer and sin do not mix.

To Save One Life

Items Needed

A chart or compilation of names of persons who have all descended from the same person.

Action During Presentation

Show the chart.

Suggested Wording for Presentation

All these people descended from this one person! But what if that original person had died as a baby? What if that person had been lost to the Church by inactivity until he had just drifted away? How many of these people would have been in the Church today?

There is a sentence in the Jewish Talmud that counsels:

"To save one life is like saving a whole nation."

If saving the life physically is important, how much greater it must be to save one life, spiritually.

To Transfer This Lesson

Items Needed

A large bottle or other container; many smaller bottles or containers.

Action During Presentation

Transfer liquid or sand or beans etc., from the large container to the smaller ones.

Suggested Wording during Presentation

When gardeners transfer seedling plants from the large bed to individual places in the garden, they carefully dig and cultivate around each individual plant. It is that way with gospel teaching too. When ideas are transplanted from the teacher's experience, or from his manual and textbook reading, to the individual, those ideas need careful transplanting. To be truly effective, we must know, and work with, each individual and his needs.

Putting it another way, suppose the material for my lesson today has been stored in this large bottle. Each of you in the same supposition is represented by one of these small containers.

My problem, of course, is to transfer the lesson material from the large container to the smaller containers in the most effective way possible. What shall I do? I could attempt to throw the "lesson material" in the general direction of the other containers, hoping that each one will get its share, and that little will be wasted. (This might be mock demon-strated if care is taken that someone's good clothes are not hurt.)

Or, it could be done in an effective way by taking time to fill each small container according to its capacity and ability to receive from the larger one.

Two Things Cannot Occupy

Items Needed

A can (a half-gallon or gallon honey can, or a tomato juice can), sand, water, rubbing alcohol.

Action During Presentation

Fill the can with sand; then over the sand pour water; next add alcohol.

Suggested Wording for Presentation

In speaking of matter, there is a physical law that two things cannot possibly occupy the same space at the same time.

But scientists are beginning to think that that physical law must be revised. Sometimes we may have two or three things occupying the same space at the same time.

There is a section in the Doctrine and Covenants, dating from May 1843, that bears out this all-important "modern viewpoint."

The Prophet Joseph Smith said:

"There is no such thing as immaterial matter. All spirit is matter, but it is more fine or pure, and can only be discerned by purer eyes;

"We cannot see it; but when our bodies are purified; we shall see that it is all matter." (D&C 131:7-8.)

You will notice that I have filled this can with sand.

(Invite members of the class to inspect the can full of sand. Have some additional sand available, if someone thinks he can get more sand into the can.)

When the sand fills the can there would seem to be no more space in the can. Yet, as I pour the water into the can, it is absorbed and a "surprising" amount of water can be added without the danger of spilling over.

Now that the sand and the water are both in the can you will probably tell me that there was probably air space between the grains of sand—air space that is now occupied by water.

This experiment could be repeated by adding the alcohol to water. An equal amount of alcohol can be added to the same amount of water, and you will have the same amount of mixture that you started out with. The alcohol could also be added to the sand and water in the can without spilling over.

If this were a real laboratory experiment perhaps the next matter to be added would be ether, which could find place in the can of sand, water and alcohol.

If we had the proper equipment and the time, each of the matters could be returned to its original form. First, the ether would be distilled out, then the alcohol, and finally the water would be distilled out, leaving the can of the dry sand that was originally started with.

The Two Sticks

Item Needed

A stick cut in two in such a way that it can be rejoined.

Action During Presentation

Show how the sticks that have been notched specially when they were cut apart can become as one stick as you fit them together.

Suggested Wording for Presentation

"Moreover, thou son of man, take thee one stick and write upon it, For Judah, and for the children of Israel his companions; then take another stick, and write upon it, For Joseph, the stick of Ephraim, and for all the house of Israel his companions:

"And join them one to another into one stick; and they shall become one in thine hand." (Ezek. 37:16-17.)

Latter-day Saints have long considered this to mean that the heritage from Judah, the Bible, and the heritage from Joseph, the Book of Mormon, are to be joined together in preaching the fulness of the gospel.

The Bible and the Book of Mormon, being the Word of God, came from a common source, and therefore should go back together as the restored gospel is presented.

But the sticks spoken of in Ezekiel?

Notice how these two sticks, though separated, can become as one. (Demonstrate with sticks.)

(Dr. Hugh Nibley of Brigham Young University, writing in The Improvement Era, January 1953, related how legal and other agreements were made in medieval England. Sticks were separated, each person taking one piece of the stick to bring it back to a perfect union, perhaps years later, when the agreement was finally completed.)

The Unthankful Heart Like a Finger

Items Needed

Magnet, and a dish of sand and iron particles mixed.

Action During Presentation

As the discussion indicates, move finger through dish of sand and iron; then sweep the magnet through the sand and iron; show how it picks up the iron.

Suggested Wording for Presentation

Our days are somewhat like this dish of sand and iron —each hour mixed with unpleasantness, with kindness, with blessings, and with hurts. As we live each day we gather to ourselves that which we seek, and that which we attract.

This is a quotation from Henry Ward Beecher, the American clergyman who lived from 1813 to 1887:

"If one should give me a dish of sand and tell me there were some particles of iron in it, I would look for the iron with my eyes and search for it with my clumsy fingers, and be unable to detect the bits of iron; but let me take a magnet and sweep through it and how it would draw to itself the almost invisible particles by the mere power of attraction. The unthankful heart, like my finger in the sand, discovers no mercies; but let the thankful heart sweep through the day, and as the magnet finds the iron, so it will find in every hour some heavenly blessings, only the iron in God's sand is gold."

Show how the magnet picks up the iron from the dish of sand as you discuss how the Lord loves a grateful heart.

Viewed From a Standpoint

Item Needed

With your camera go hunting for a good horizon or landscape. Take two pictures; in one deliberately set your camera for a "close-up." Then take the same view with your camera lens properly set.

Action During Presentation

Use the two pictures to begin the discussion; show how the set of the lens for the different view caused the difference in pictures.

Suggested Wording for Presentation

(Discuss the pictures with the class.) When we look at the two pictures, we are aware that there is nothing wrong with the horizon or the landscape that we photographed. It was the same all the time. It was the set of our view that left one photograph with much to be desired.

We often do the same thing in considering the things of God. We consider the program as a "close-up" when in reality it should be viewed from a standpoint of infinity.

Surely, "He who made all things will judge all things."

In the Sermon on the Mount, Jesus said:

"Lay not up for yourselves treasures upon earth, where moth and rust doth corrupt, and where thieves break through and steal;

106

"But lay up for yourselves treasures in heaven, where neither moth nor rust doth corrupt, and where thieves do not break through nor steal;

"For where your treasure is, there will your heart be also." (Matt. 6:19-21.)

At another time he said:

"If any man will come after me, let him deny himself, and take up his cross, and follow me.

"For whosoever will save his life shall lose it; and whosoever will lose his life for my sake shall find it.

"For, what is a man profited, if he shall gain the whole world, and lose his own soul? or what shall a man give in exchange for his soul?" (Matt. 16:24-26.)

We Nourish Our Faith

Items Needed

Newspaper and scissors. If it is green newsprint, so much the better.

Action During Presentation

Roll the newspaper up into a roll, one sheet at a time, and overlapping the sheets several inches. Now, cut, or tear, from one end, making several strips about half way to the other end. Grasp the inside firmly and pull out on it toward the out ends. It will take practice before you face an audience, but you can produce a very tall "tree" that "grows" right before the eyes as you speak.

Suggested Wording for Presentation

The Book of Alma in the Book of Mormon records many important facets of the gospel. Chapter 32, verses 25 to 42 is a great discussion on faith. There Alma said: "We will compare the word unto a seed. . . ." (Verse 28.)

Continuing, he told that the seed would grow if given a place in the heart and nourished. "The tree beginneth to grow . . . if ye nourish it with much care it will get root, and grow up, and bring forth fruit." (Verse 37.)

(Demonstrate with newspaper how the tree grows.)

We nourish our faith by the study of the scriptures, by prayer, and by obedience to the laws of the gospel. Our faith grows and we begin to produce "fruit," the fruits of the Spirit become part of our own lives, and even testimonies in others are born through our words and deeds.

To See Ourselves

Item Needed

Mirror

Action During Presentation

Show mirror up to class; let members see themselves if possible.

Suggested Wording during Presentation

Does a mirror ever give us a true likeness of ourselves? A special mirror perhaps does. But a common mirror throws our reflection back at us in reverse. You can check that by glancing at your watch or a clock in the mirror. Still, we are so used to seeing ourselves the way the mirror shows us that few of us would recognize ourselves any other way. We therefore see ourselves in our own light, and not as anyone else sees us.

Robert Burns in his poem, "To A Louse," rhymed:

"O wad some Pow'r the giftie gie us
To see oursels as ithers see us!
It wad frae monie a blunder free us. . . ."

Indeed it would from many a blunder free us, if we could see ourselves as others do.

But the great truth that we all should seek is for a glimpse of ourselves as seen in the sight of God. That would be most revealing. It, too, ought to be most helpful. But we do not walk alone. Neither do we need to walk with a reverse image. We have His commandments to guide us.

What Does Your Mind Picture?

Items Needed

Piece of paper, scissors

Action During Presentation

Take a single sheet of paper; fold it in half. Then fold it in halves again with a fold parallel to the first fold. Cut through the last fold with scissors. When these directions are actually followed, the experiment ends with three pieces of paper.

Suggested Wording for Presentation

How photographic is your mind? What does your mind picture as we discuss a principle of the gospel? Sometimes it is very difficult to get the same idea over to members of the same group as they listen and study together.

How photographic is your mind? For a moment, let's experiment with something completely unrelated to religion.

Suppose you have a single sheet of paper. (Demonstrate.) Fold it in halves. Then fold it in halves again with a fold parallel to the first fold.

Then suppose you were to cut through the last fold with scissors. How many pieces of paper would you have?

What Is the Size?

Items Needed

A book and tape measure

Action During Presentation

At the beginning, hold the book up to the class and have them estimate its size. At the end of the discussion, measure the book.

Suggested Wording for Presentation

"What is the size of this book, in inches? How high do you think it is? How wide is it?" (Have people estimate and hold their figures in reserve.)

Few people have ever seen the Book of Mormon plates. The Book of Mormon records the solemn statements of eleven men, the three witnesses, and the eight witnesses, and the twelfth man would be the Prophet, Joseph Smith.

How large were the Plates? Joseph Smith, writing the Wentworth letter, says they "had the appearance of gold, each plate was six inches wide and eight inches long, and not quite so thick as common tin." (*Documentary History of the Church,* Vol. 4, p. 537.)

David Whitmer, according to the book *The Prophet of Palmyra,* was interviewed by the *Kansas City Journal* shortly before his death, saying:

"They appeared to be of gold, about six by nine inches

in size, about as thick as parchment." (There is some doubt that this interview took place.)

Martin Harris, another of the three witnesses, according to *Myth of the Manuscript Found*, estimated the plates at eight by seven inches and the thickness of the volume at four inches, each plate being as thick as thick tin.

Orson Pratt had not seen the plates himself, but had an inquiring mind and knew those who had seen the plates. He tells in *Remarkable Visions* that the plates were eight by seven inches, and that the entire volume was about six inches, while each plate was about as thick as common tin. Orson Pratt also says that two-thirds of the plates were sealed.

Joseph Smith, six by eight inches. David Whitmer, six by nine. Martin Harris, eight by seven. Orson Pratt, eight by seven. These were honest men who never thought to measure the plates. The fact that there is a slight variance adds credence to the story of the plates. Had the story been a fabrication, then there would have in all likelihood been a constant measurement figure.

(Give the measurements of the book as you measure it.) How good were your eyes?

Will a Man Rob God?

Items Needed

Ten objects of equal value—apples, coins, or the like.

Action During Presentation

Indicate the ten objects; as discussion proceeds, separate them one by one.

Suggested Wording for Presentation

Suppose your earnings for a month amounted to these. And you had promised to pay a tenth, or one of these, as a tithing. How easy it is to pay the first and have nine left.

But when the first goes to the landlord, and the second goes to the grocer, and the third goes to that good-natured fellow at the service station, and the fourth goes to the baker, and the fifth, and the sixth, and the seventh, just go. . . .

Suddenly the realization that there is but one left comes to you. How much harder it is at that moment to give the remaining one as tithing. Too often at that moment such a person by default joins the kind of people who were admonished by Malachi, the last of the recorded Old Testament prophets:

"Will a man rob God? Yet ye have robbed me. But ye say, Wherein have we robbed thee? In tithes and offerings.

"Ye are cursed with a curse; for ye have robbed me, even this whole nation.

114

"Bring ye all the tithes into the storehouse, that there may be meat in mine house, and prove me now herewith, saith the Lord of hosts, if I will not open the windows of heaven, and pour you out a blessing, that there shall not be room enough to receive it." (Mal. 3:8-10.)

A Window of Understanding

Items Needed

A blank piece of paper; a pencil

Action During Presentation

Hold the paper to the class to show how blank it is; use pencil to write on the paper when the discussion calls for it.

Suggested Wording for Presentation

What do you see? Be truthful now. Some of you say you see a blank piece of paper. Good, you see in the present. But that gives some of you a window of understanding. Some of you now see the paper mill from whence the paper came, and perhaps the majestic tree of the forest. That's good, if this paper is one hundred percent wood pulp. What if it is a grade of paper that has a rag content?

Now, what if a pencil is placed with the paper. Certainly we can trace the pencil in the same way that the paper was traced. But now let's look for possibilities in the future. A grocery list? A hurried note left on the kitchen table to not let the meal in the oven burn? Or perhaps even a sonnet that will rival Shakespeare's ability, or some music the likes of which the world hasn't seen since Beethoven? What do you see?

Pilate, the Roman representative in Jerusalem, countered the Christ with:

"What is truth?" (John 18:38.)

Since that time libraries have been filled with men's definitions to that question, "What is truth?"

We like the definition given through revelation to the Prophet Joseph Smith: "And truth is knowledge of things as they are, and as they were, and as they are to come." (D&C 93:24.)

What Is the Difference?

Items Needed

A coin and a disc the same size cut from cardboard.

Action During Presentation

Show the genuine coin and the cardboard disc when needed.

Suggested Wording for Presentation

You all know what this is. It is a coin that is genuine and can be spent anywhere in our great land. But what is this? Yes, it is a piece of cardboard. What makes it different from the coin? It is the same shape. It is the same weight. We could take a coloring pencil and make it the same color. What is the difference? Yes, the coin was made in a mint, having authority, and the coin is so marked as the official coin of the realm, and can so act.

Every day of our lives we fill with many acts. As we live our lives through, let's make sure that we are genuine, and our acts are as they are intended to be.

Without a Pure Point

Items Needed

Your own two feet

Action During Presentation

Keeping one foot steady, stand and swing the other foot or move it in a full arc.

Suggested Wording for Presentation

You have probably used this demonstration often in your high school geometry class. Let's apply the principle of the compass to teach an eternal truth.

Place one foot so that it does not move. The other foot may swing in a wide circle, move at a narrow angle, or a wide angle; but as long as the one foot remains fixed, the circle will always remain true.

Now, without a sure point of reference you may stray and your life may never form the perfect circle, but as long as God remains as the center you can be sure that your circle will be just and true. You will have a complete life, rather than an irregular, purposeless existence.

Would It Be Honored?

Items Needed

A paper dollar, a piece of scratch paper about that size.

Action During Presentation

Show the paper dollar and the scratch paper at beginning of discussion.

Suggested Wording for Discussion

This dollar bill is genuine. It has the proper signature and the other markings on it that make it acceptable anywhere. But what if I were to take a piece of scratch paper and attempt to make my own money? What would be the consequences? Would it be honored? Would it have authority?

The world acts this way sometimes in administering the ordinance of baptism and the other very necessary ordinances of the gospel. Where is their authority? Their piece of paper is not genuine.

Seeking wisdom in the Spring of 1820, fourteen-year-old Joseph Smith prayed in a secluded grove in upstate New York. His petition was answered by his glorious First Vision of the Father and the Son. In April 1830 the gospel was restored through him as The Church of Jesus Christ of Latter-day Saints was again organized and began to function among men and women upon the earth. The Church has the Priesthood operating within it—the divine authority so necessary. The fifth Article of Faith of the Church states:

"We believe that a man must be called of God, by prophecy, and by the laying on of hands, by those who are in authority to preach the Gospel and administer in the ordinances thereof."

Truly, The Church of Jesus Christ of Latter-day Saints is the only organization upon the face of the earth whose power and authority is recognized in heaven.

Would You Be Able?

Items Needed

Find out from your bishop the per capita fast offerings given in your ward. Purchase from the store what the per capita amount for fast offering would buy for one meal.

Action During Presentation

Show the purchase and the figures on the fast offering per capita.

Suggested Wording for Presentation

Would you like to be able to live on such a meal? Still, by your fast offerings you think that such a meal will be adequate. Well, how about it?

Speaking of the sanctity of the Sabbath, the Lord said in the Doctrine and Covenants:

"And on this day thou shalt do none other thing, only let thy food be prepared with singleness of heart that thy fasting may be perfect, or, in other words, that thy joy may be full.

"Verily, this is fasting and prayer, or in other words, rejoicing and prayer.

"Verily, I say, that inasmuch as ye do this, the fulness of the earth is yours." (D&C 59:13-14, 16.)

Could anyone ever ask for more?

We See Only the Underneath Part

Items Needed

Telescope or a picture of the heavens on a starry night.

Actions During Presentation

Show the picture of the heavens, or if possible look through telescope.

Suggested Wording for Presentation

When one looks into the heavens one stands in profound awe at its beauty. As a little child once said: "Heaven must be beautiful, because it looks so nice when we see only the underneath part."

The naked eye sees thousands of stars, each a sun, many of them rivalling our own sun in size and brilliance. The telescope gives us power to see beyond the ability of our own eyesight. And the radio telescope extends our horizon even further.

But no one has ever encompassed the end of space. William W. Phelps, one of our latter-day hymnists, sang from the bottom of his soul, these words:

If You Could Hie to Kolob

If you could hie to Kolob
In the twinkling of an eye,
And then continue onward
With that same speed to fly,

D'ye think that you could ever,
Through all eternity,
Find out the generation
Where Gods began to be?

Or see the grand beginning
Where space did not extend?
Or view the last creation,
Where Gods and matter end?
Methinks the Spirit whispers,
"No man has found 'pure space,' "
Nor seen the outside curtains,
Where nothing has a place.

The works of God continue,
And worlds and lives abound;
Improvement and progression
Have one eternal round.
There is no end to matter;
There is no end to space;
There is no end to spirit;
There is no end to race.

There is no end to virtue;
There is no end to might;
There is no end to wisdom;
There is no end to light;
There is no end to union;
There is no end to youth;
There is no end to priesthood;
There is no end to truth.

There is no end to glory;
There is no end to love;
There is no end to being;
There is no death above. . . .

What is the purpose of all this? The stars above and the
earth beneath? It is all for the glory of man.

As the Psalmist was inspired:

"When I consider thy heavens, the work of thy fingers, the moon and the stars, which thou hast ordained;

"What is man, that thou art mindful of him? and the son of man, that thou visitest him?

"For thou hast made him a little lower than the angels, and hast crowned him with glory and honour.

"Thou madest him to have dominion over the works of thy hands; thou hast put all things under his feet." (Psalm 8:3-6.)

Surely we see the handiwork of the Creator everywhere we look.

You Always Take With You

Items Needed

A dead "coal" from the fireplace.

Action During Presentation

Show the black dead coal. Pick it up and demonstrate the black that remains on the hands.

Suggested Wording for Presentation

Just a while ago this coal was red hot. It would have been foolish for anyone to have picked it up then with bare hands. But now that the flame and fire have died away, can we safely touch it? Can we safely touch sin after the flame and the fire have died away?

No, no matter how carefully you try to touch this coal, you always take with you some of its tell-tale black marks.

There is said to be in the Mint a delicate set of scales that is used to weigh the precious metals used in the coinage of the nation's money. Those who are invited to see the Mint in operation see that scales and some are invited to make a mark upon a piece of paper that will be so slight that the delicate scales will not detect it. Some practically invisible marks are made, but the scales always detect them by recording a difference in weight.

The metals of the earth are precious in the sight of men, but how much more precious are the men of the earth in the sight of God?

In interpreting the dream of Belshazzar, one of the great men of the ancient world, Daniel, one of the young prophets of Israel, said,

"Thou art weighed in the balances, and art found wanting." (Dan. 5:27.)

The Lord weighs an individual for good or bad.

How close can we get to this dead coal without being marked with its dirt and blackness? We can't touch it at all, either accidentally or purposely.

In modern revelation the Lord has said, "I, the Lord, am bound when ye do what I say; but when ye do not what I say, ye have no promise." (D&C 82:10.) and ". . .I . . .cannot look upon sin with the least degree of allowance." (D&C 1:31.)